Collector's Guide to the
EPIDOTE GROUP

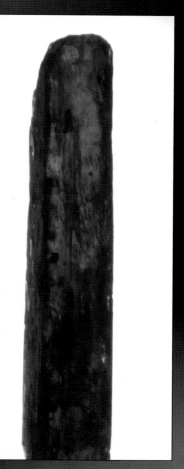

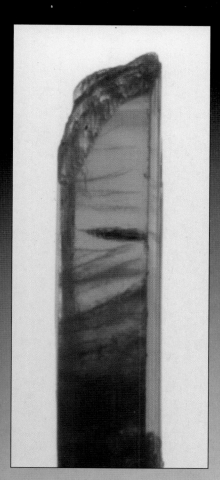

Schiffer Earth Science Monographs Volume 2

Schiffer Publishing Ltd

4880 Lower Valley Road, Atglen, Pennsylvania 19310

Robert J. Lauf

Other Schiffer Books by Robert J. Lauf
Collector's Guide to the Mica Group: Schiffer Earth Science Monographs Volume 1.
Introduction to Radioactive Minerals.

Other Schiffer Books on Related Subjects
Collecting Fluorescent Minerals. Stuart Schneider
The World of Fluorescent Minerals. Stuart Schneider

Designed by Mark David Bowyer
Type set in Arno Pro / Humanist 521 BT

ISBN: 978-0-7643-3048-3
Printed in China

Schiffer Books are available at special discounts for bulk purchases for sales promotions or premiums. Special editions, including personalized covers, corporate imprints, and excerpts can be created in large quantities for special needs. For more information contact the publisher:

Published by Schiffer Publishing Ltd.
4880 Lower Valley Road
Atglen, PA 19310
Phone: (610) 593-1777; Fax: (610) 593-2002
E-mail: Info@schifferbooks.com

Please visit our web site catalog at **www.schifferbooks.com**

We are always looking for people to write books on new and related subjects. If you have an idea for a book, please contact us at the above address.

This book may be purchased from the publisher.
Include $5.00 for shipping.
Please try your bookstore first.
You may write for a free catalog.

In Europe, Schiffer books are distributed by:
Bushwood Books
6 Marksbury Ave.
Kew Gardens
Surrey TW9 4JF
England
Phone: 44 (0)208 392-8585
Fax: 44 (0)208 392-9876
E-mail: Info@bushwoodbooks.co.uk

Website: www.bushwoodbooks.co.uk
Free postage in the UK. Europe: air mail at cost.
Try your bookstore first.

Contents

Preface

This volume continues a series of monographs on important groups of so-called rock forming silicates, the purpose of which is to help mineral collectors gain a better appreciation of these complex minerals. Because of the importance of rock forming minerals in geological processes, they are the subject of extensive published research, much of which has been brought together in the five-volume compendium *Rock-Forming Minerals* (Deer, Howie, and Zussman 1962) and the greatly expanded Second Edition thereof. Among rock-forming minerals, the epidote group is well known to collectors because several members of the group (epidote in particular) often form spectacular crystals and aesthetic combination specimens with other minerals. New sources of outstanding specimens in China and Pakistan are destined to become "classic localities" in the future. Some members of the group (and the related mineral zoisite) are important gem and lapidary materials. The author considers it especially timely to take a detailed look at the epidote group because the nomenclature of the group has recently been clarified by a committee of the IMA and the names of several species have been changed.

This monograph is organized as follows: After a brief introduction, the general treatment begins with an explanation of the chemistry and taxonomy of the group with supporting tables to illustrate the logic of their classification and relationships to one another. A section on their formation and geochemistry explains the kinds of environments where epidotes can form. Then, a detailed entry for each mineral provides extensive locality information and full-color photos wherever possible so that collectors can see what good specimens look like and which minerals one might expect to find in association with epidotes.

Acknowledgments

The author is especially grateful to Thomas Armbruster of the University of Bern, Switzerland, for providing a draft copy of the paper on epidote nomenclature. The following colleagues kindly provided technical information, literature, and helpful discussions: Deborah Cole, *Oak Ridge National Laboratory*; Frank Hawthorne, *University of Manitoba*; Tony Kampf, *L.A. County Museum*; Tom Watkins, *Oak Ridge National Laboratory*. Important specimens and background information were supplied by Dudley Blauwet, *Mountain Minerals International*; Dave Bunk; Sharon Cisneros, *Mineralogical Research Co.*; Richard Dale, *Dale Minerals*; Jordi Fabre, *Fabre Minerals*; Leonard Himes, *Minerals America*; Rob Kulakofski, *Color-Wright*; David Lare, *Jeffrey Mining Co.*; Tom Loomis, *Dakota Matrix Minerals*; Neal Pfaff, *M. Phantom Minerals*; C. Carter Rich; Brian Stefanek, *Universal Rock Shop*; Russ Underwood, *J R Rocks*; Chris Wright, *Wright's Rock Shop*.

Introduction

The epidote group consists of eighteen minerals, of which epidote, clinozoisite, and the allanite series are best known to collectors. Many of these minerals form well-crystallized specimens, often with interesting associates, ranging from superb micromounts to spectacular decorator pieces. Allanites are of particular interest to collectors of radioactive species and rare-earth minerals. Zoisite, the orthorhombic polymorph of clinozoisite, is an important gem mineral for faceting, and massive zoisite is a familiar lapidary material. Zoisite is included here even though it is no longer a member of the group according to recently approved nomenclature.

History of the group

Epidote was first named and described by Haüy at the beginning of the nineteenth century, a time when X-ray crystallography was not yet known. At the time, minerals were distinguished from one another by properties such as crystal morphology, color and other optical properties, density, etc., that a keen observer could actually determine with the available tools. A number of other names were rejected at the time because they referred either to specific color variants or specific localities. The name clinozoisite was applied by Weinschenck in 1896 to iron-poor epidote found at Prägratten, Austria, in recognition that it was the monoclinic dimorph of zoisite, which had been described by Werner in 1805. (Zoisite was the only orthorhombic mineral that was originally placed in the epidote group; all the others are isostructural with epidote.) The manganese epidote, piemontite, was described by Kenngott in 1853 based on material from the Praborna mine, Italy; however, without modern analytical techniques the name was applied to generally red, pleochroic epidotes without regard for "modern" concepts of how mineral species within a group are differentiated. Rare-earth element (REE) bearing epidotes were recognized early on with the description of allanite by Thomson in 1811. In addition to these early species, there was a proliferation of varietal names based on color or compositional variations. Some of these names include: *fouqueite*, *pistacite*, *orthite*, *tawmawite*, *thulite*, and *withamite*.

The morphology of epidote was exhaustively documented by Goldschmidt (1916), who illustrated 372 drawings of epidote crystals and 18 drawings of zoisite crystals.

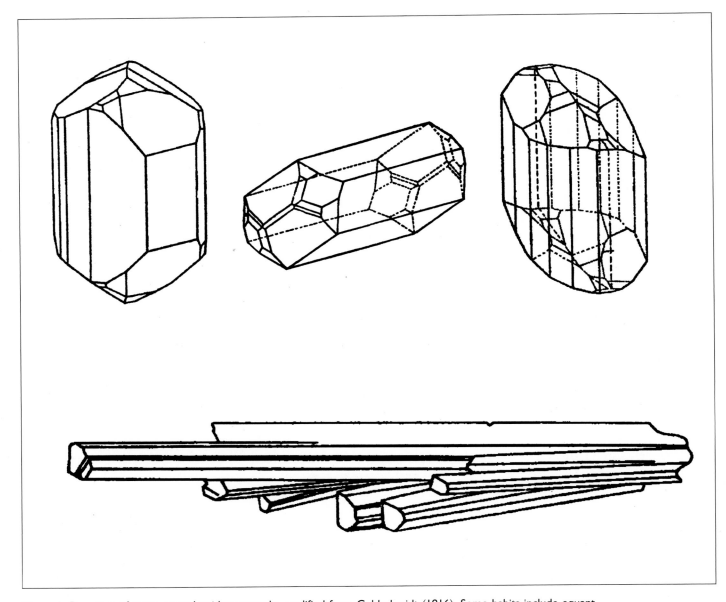

Figure 1. Drawings of some natural epidote crystals, modified from Goldschmidt (1916). Some habits include equant to tabular single crystals showing numerous forms (faces representing various crystallographic planes) and a spray of elongated crystals in sub-parallel arrangement.

Gem and lapidary uses

Transparent, defect-free or "faceting grade" epidote crystals are not particularly rare, but over-all their appeal as a faceting material is limited by two factors. First, with a Mohs hardness of 6.5, epidote is softer than most familiar gemstones. Second, much of it is too dark to cut very large stones and because of its pleochroism the finished stones are often fairly unattractive shades of green-ish brown. Cabochons are occasionally cut from quartz that is colored by inclusions of epidote. Another useful lapidary material is *unakite*, a mot-tled green-pink epidosite. Some epidotes contain fibrous inclusions and can be cut into "cat's-eye" type cabochons.

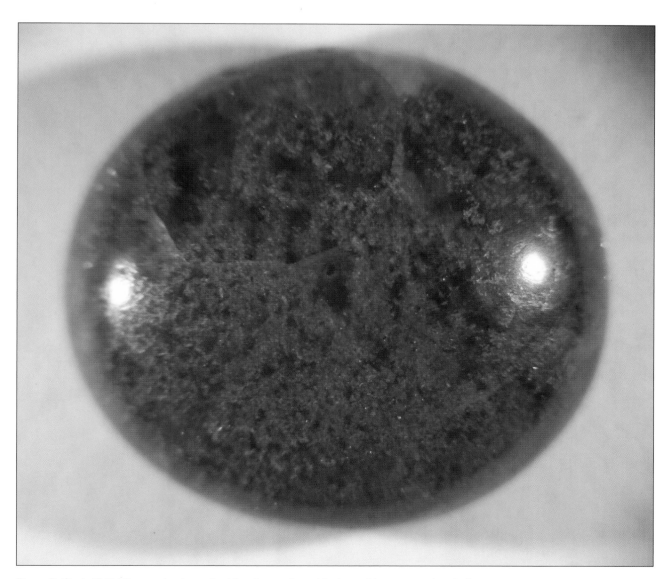

Figure 2. Oval, 15 X 17 mm cabochon of epidote/quartz from Mexico, with a green color similar to moss agate.

Figure 3. Slab of unakite from Max Patch, Tennessee. This sample is mostly green epidote with a small amount of other minerals, including pink feldspar. RJL3185

Figure 4. Tumble-polished freeform pieces of unakite from China, showing the rich color and high polish that makes the material popular with lapidaries.

Figure 5. Jewelry set made with a tasteful combination of unakite and silver wire-wrap mounting technique.

Figure 6. Chinese unakite carved in the shape of a dragon. The carving is about 8 cm tall.

Among the minerals discussed in this book, the most commercially important gemstone is the sapphire-blue zoisite called *tanzanite*. The material is found in the Merelani area of Tanzania where it forms in calc-silicate rocks, believed to be of hydrothermal origin, associated with graphitic gneiss. Most of the crystals are brownish when mined and the blue color is obtained by heat treatment at 400–650°C. Both raw and heat treated stones are usually noticeably pleochroic. Heat-treated stones do not always end up with the desired deep blue color but may be colorless or various shades of bluish-green, yellow, or pink.

Figure 7. Blue zoisite var. *tanzanite* crystal about 1 cm tall from Arusha, Tanzania. Heat treatment was undoubtedly used to enhance the blue color. RJL1034

Some green zoisite is transparent enough to facet but by far the more familiar form to lapidaries is a massive green chromian variety containing opaque but very bright red ruby crystals from Longido, Tanzania. "Ruby in zoisite" is a fairly unique metamorphic rock consisting of light green zoisite, black sodium-rich amphibole, and ruby. The local name for it is *anyolite* taken from the Masai word for "green." Many tons of it has been mined starting from the mid-1950s (Keller 1992). The rock is very colorful and is a popular subject for carving as well as fashioning into cabochons, spheres, and eggs. When cutting and polishing, some care is needed to allow for the difference in hardness between the ruby crystals and the matrix. The pink variety of zoisite, called *thulite*, is rarely transparent enough to facet, but massive material makes excellent rich pink cabochons.

Figure 8. Large, well-formed hexagonal ruby crystal in green zoisite var. *anyolite*, from Tanzania. The ruby is about 6 cm across. RJL2129

Figure 9. Richly colored pink slab of zoisite var. *thulite* suitable for cutting cabochons, from Leksvik, Norway. RJL3183

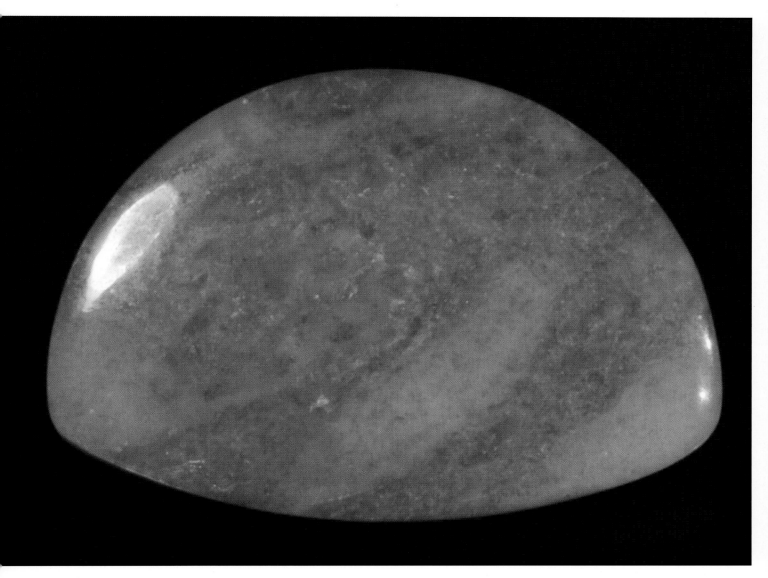

Figure 10. Polished freeform cabochon of zoisite var. *thulite* 35 X 50 mm, from Leksvik, Norway.

Taxonomy of the Epidote Group

The epidote group has suffered over the years from a lack of universally accepted nomenclature (Deer, Howie, and Zussman 1986) and an over-abundance of names, such as *fouqueite*, *pistacite*, *puschkinite*, and *withamite*, to list just a few. Furthermore, the REE-bearing epidotes were a particularly confusing group as discussed in the aptly titled paper, "The Mess that is Allanite" (Ercit 2002). In an attempt to bring some accepted order to this group, the Commission on New Minerals and Mineral Names of the International Mineralogical Association established a Subcommittee on Epidote-Group Mineral Nomenclature. The result of that work was to create an officially accepted list of known valid species as well as a framework for classifying (and naming) possible new species as they are discovered. The following synopsis is taken from that report (Armbruster et al. 2006):

General formula

Members of the group as now defined are monoclinic silicates (space group $P2_1/m$) whose general formula may be summarized as follows:

$$\mathbf{A1A2M1M2M3}[Si_2O_7][SiO_4](\mathbf{O4})(\mathbf{O10})$$

where:

A1 is Ca;
A2 is Ca, REE, Pb, Sr;
M1 is Al, Fe, Mg, Mn;
M2 is Al;
M3 is Al, Fe^{3+}, Mn^{3+}, V^{3+}, Cr^{3+};
O4 is O^{2-}, F^-; and
O10 is OH^-, O^{2-}.

Crystal structure

Referring to the general formula shown above, the crystal structure may be described as follows: The monoclinic structure consists of Si_2O_7 and SiO_4 units linked to two kinds of chains (parallel to the *b*-axis of the crystal) built from edge-sharing octahedra. One chain comprises the **M2** octahedra and the other chain is formed by **M1** octahedra with **M3** octahedra attached on alternate sides along its length. The **M** octahedra are generally occupied by trivalent ions (e.g., Al, Fe^{3+}, Mn^{3+}, Cr^{3+}, V^{3+}). Divalent ions such as Mg, Fe^{2+}, and Mn^{2+} may occupy **M** sites (with a preference for **M3**) if heterovalent substitutions are involved. **M2** has a strong preference for Al whereas **M1** and **M3** occupancy depends on competing ions. An OH^- group is usually bonded to the **M2** cation. Overall the structural arrangement gives rise to two types of cavities, a smaller one designated **A1**, usually occupied by Ca or Mn^{2+}, and a larger one designated **A2**, usually occupied by Ca, Sr, Pb, or REE. The resulting topology is consistent with space group $P2_1/m$. This structure contains ten symmetry independent anion sites designated **O1** – **O10**. In natural materials **O10** typically represents OH^- whereas the **O4** site may be occupied by O^{2-} in the clinozoisite and allanite subgroups or by F^- in the dollaseite subgroup. Formulas for all presently accepted species are given in Table 1.

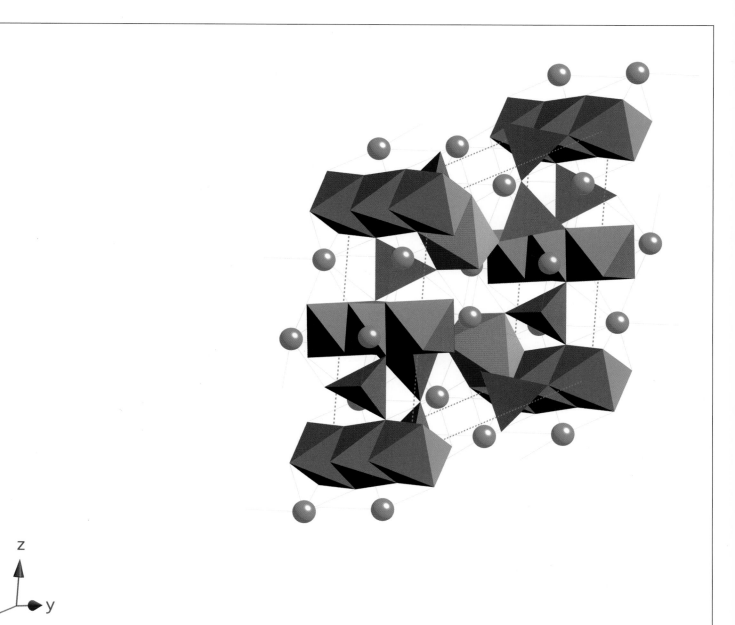

Figure 11. The crystal structure of epidote. In this type of model, each coordination polyhedron represents a metal ion (hidden within the polyhedron) surrounded by oxygen ions at the corners. For better visualization, the Ca ions occupying the **A1** and **A2** sites are shown here as green spheres rather than as coordination polyhedra. Purple tetrahedra represent (SiO_4) groups; blue octahedra represent the **M1** and **M2** sites occupied by Al; yellow octahedra represent the **M3** site occupied by Fe. In order to better emphasize the periodic structure, the model shows more than just a single unit cell.

Tables of species and their formulas

Table 1. Mineral species in the Epidote Group

Name	Formula	Symmetry
Allanite-(Ce)	$(Ca,Ce,La)_2(Al,Fe^{2+},Fe^{3+})_3Si_3O_{12}(OH)$	mon
Allanite-(La)	$(La,Y,Ca)_2(Al,Fe^{3+})_3Si_3O_{12}(OH)$	mon
Allanite-(Y)	$(Y,Ce,Ca)_2(Al,Fe^{3+})_3Si_3O_{12}(OH)$	mon
Clinozoisite	$Ca_2Al_3Si_3O_{12}(OH)$	mon
Clinozoisite-(Sr)	$CaSrAl_3Si_3O_{12}(OH)$	mon
Dissakisite-(Ce)	$Ca(Ce,La)MgAl_2(SiO_4)_3(OH)$	mon
Dissakisite-(La)	$Ca(La,Ce)MgAl_2(SiO_4)_3(OH)$	mon
Dollaseite-(Ce)	$CaCeMg_2AlSi_3O_{11}(F,OH)_2$	mon
Epidote	$Ca_2Al_2(Fe^{3+},Al)Si_3O_{12}(OH)$	mon
Epidote-(Pb)	$(Pb,Ca,Sr)_2(Al,Fe^{3+})_3Si_3O_{12}(OH)$	mon
Epidote-(Sr)[a]	$CaSrAl_2Fe^{3+}Si_3O_{12}(OH)$	mon
Khristovite-(Ce)	$(Ca,REE)REE(Mg,Fe^{2+})AlMn^{2+}Si_3O_{11}$ (OH)(F,O)	mon
Mukhinite	$Ca_2Al_2V^{3+}Si_3O_{12}(OH)$	mon
Mangani-piemontite-(Sr)	$CaSrMn^{3+}AlMn^{3+}Si_3O_{11}O(OH)$	mon
Mangani-androsite-(Ce)	$(Mn^{2+},Ca)(Ce,REE)Mn^{3+}AlMn^{2+}Si_3O_{11}O(OH)$	mon
Mangani-androsite-(La)	$Mn^{2+}La Mn^{3+}AlMn^{2+}Si_3O_{11}O(OH)$	mon
Piemontite	$Ca_2(Al,Mn^{3+},Fe^{3+})_3Si_3O_{12}(OH)$	mon
Piemontite-(Sr)	$CaSr(Al,Mn^{3+},Fe^{3+})_3Si_3O_{11}O(OH)$	mon
Vanado-androsite-(Ce)	$Mn^{2+}CeV^{3+}AlMn^{2+}Si_3O_{11}O(OH)$	mon
Zoisite[b]	$Ca_2Al_3Si_3O_{12}(OH)$	orth

[a]Recommended name (Armbruster et al. 2006) for Fe-rich analogue of clinozoisite-(Sr) if/when such species is found and formally described.
[b]Not a member of the group as now defined.

The epidote group is now further divided into three subgroups:

(1) Members of the **clinozoisite subgroup** are derived from the mineral clinozoisite $Ca_2Al_3[Si_2O_7]$ $[SiO_4]O(OH)$ by homovalent substitutions only. The key cation- and anion-sites are $A1 = M^{2+}$, $A2 = M^{2+}$, $M1 = M^{3+}$, $M2 = M^{3+}$, $M3 = M^{3+}$, $O4 = O^{2-}$, $O10 = (OH)^-$. In other words, the **A1** and **A2** sites will be occupied by divalent metal ions, the **M1**, **M2**, and **M3** sites will be occupied by trivalent metal ions, the **O4** site will contain oxygen, and the **O10** site will contain the hydroxyl ion.

(2) Members of the **allanite subgroup** are REE-rich minerals exemplified by the mineral "allanite." This subgroup may be derived from clinozoisite by homovalent substitutions and **one** coupled heterovalent substitution of the type $^{A2}(REE)^{3+} + {}^{M3}M^{2+} \rightarrow {}^{A2}Ca^{2+} + {}^{M3}M^{3+}$. In other words, a *trivalent* REE ion on a normally *divalent* **A2** site is compensated by a *divalent* ion on a normally *trivalent* **M3** site. Thus the valences on the key sites are: $A1 = M^{2+}$, **A2 = M^{3+}**, $M1 = M^{3+}$, $M2 = M^{3+}$, **M3 = M^{2+}**, $O4 = O^{2-}$, $O10 = (OH)^-$.

(3) Members of the **dollaseite subgroup** are REE-rich minerals exemplified by the mineral "dollaseite." This subgroup may be derived from clinozoisite by homovalent substitutions and **two** coupled heterovalent substitutions of the type $^{A2}(REE)^{3+} + {}^{M3}M^{2+} \rightarrow {}^{A2}Ca^{2+} + {}^{M3}M^{3+}$ and $^{M1}M^{2+} + {}^{O4}F^- \rightarrow {}^{M1}M^{3+} + {}^{O4}O^{2-}$. In other words, the first coupled substitution is the same as that shown above in the allanites, and the second substitution involves a *divalent* ion on the normally *trivalent* **M1** site compensated by substitution of *monovalent* F^- for *divalent* O^{2-} on the **O4** site. Thus the valences on the key sites are: $A1 = M^{2+}$, **A2 = M^{3+}**, **M1 = M^{2+}**, $M2 = M^{3+}$, **M3 = M^{2+}**, **O4 = F$^-$**, $O10 = (OH)^-$.

While this may seem confusing to the average collector, it provides a logical system to define particular mineral species in terms of their unique *structures* and not just on their bulk *compositions*. Under this system, the root name of a particular species will be determined by which metal ions occupy the cation sites **M3** and **A1** (and, in principle, **M2** as well). In both clinozoisite and allanite subgroups no prefix is added to the root name if **M1** = Al. If the **M1** site is dominantly occupied by Fe^{3+}, Mn^{3+}, Cr^{3+}, and V^{3+} it will be denoted by the prefixes ferri, mangani, chromo, and vanado, respectively. In the dollaseite subgroup no prefix is added to the root name if **M1** = Mg. Otherwise a proper prefix must be attached; the prefixes ferro and mangano indicate dominant Fe^{2+} and Mn^{2+} at **M1**, respectively. The dominant cation on **A2** (other than Ca) is treated according to the *Extended Levinson* suffix designation. Table 2 shows ideal compositions for all of the known minerals by subgroup in terms of the ions that occupy each site in the structure. Careful study of this table will make the logic of the classification rules clear.

Table 2. Accepted mineral species defined by the dominant ions occupying the indicated sites in the structure (Armbruster et al. 2006).

Name	A1	A2	M1	M2	M3	O4	O10
Clinozoisite Subgroup							
Clinozoisite	Ca	Ca	Al	Al	Al	O	OH
Clinozoisite-(Sr)[a,c]	Ca	Sr	Al	Al	Al	O	OH
Epidote	Ca	Ca	Al	AL	Fe^{3+}	O	OH
Epidote-(Pb)[a,d]	Ca	Pb	Al	Al	Fe^{3+}	O	OH
Mukhinite	Ca	Ca	Al	Al	V^{3+}	O	OH
Piemontite	Ca	Ca	Al	Al	Mn^{3+}	O	OH
Mangani-piemontite-(Sr)[a,f]	Ca	Sr	Mn^{3+}	Al	Mn^{3+}	O	OH
Allanite Subgroup							
Allanite-(Ce), -(La), -(Y)	Ca	REE^{3+}	Al	Al	Fe^{2+}	O	OH
Ferriallanite-(Ce)	Ca	REE^{3+}	Fe^{3+}	Al	Fe^{2+}	O	OH
Dissakisite -(Ce),-(La)	Ca	REE^{3+}	Fe^{3+}	Al	Mg	O	OH
Manganian-drosite -(La)[a,g], -(Ce)[b,g]	Mn^{2+}	REE^{3+}	Mn^{3+}	Al	Mn^{2+}	O	OH
Vanado-androsite-(Ce)[b]	Mn^{2+}	REE^{3+}	V^{3+}	Al	Mn^{2+}	O	OH
Dollaseite Subgroup							
Dollaseite-(Ce)	Ca	Ce^{3+}	Mg	Al	Mg	F	OH
Khristovite-(Ce)	Ca	Ce^{3+}	Mg	Al	Mn^{2+}	F	OH

[a]Recommended new mineral names for accepted species
[b]Approved by CNMMN (Cenki-Tok et al., 2006); vanadoandrosite-(Ce) was originally approved as vanadio-androsite-(Ce)
[c]Old name = niigataite
[d]Old name = hancockite
[e]Old name = strontiopiemontite
[f]Old name = tweddillite
[g]Old name = androsite

As noted in the footnotes to Table 2, one upshot of rationalizing the nomenclature was to change the names of some existing species. This decision has provoked some controversy on the grounds that a fundamental tenet of taxonomy in every field is that the first published name has priority; *changing* the name of a valid existing species is very different from *discrediting* a name that had been used for a now-invalid species. Nevertheless, the name changes were defended as reasonable in the interest of placing the group into a logical structural framework and it was noted that many of the renamed species were either very recently described (e.g., *tweddillite*) and/or uncommon to begin with (e.g., *hancockite*). Systematic collectors who are especially interested in rare species need to be aware of these changes, and also be aware that some dealers and older labels might still show the old name:

Niigataite is now clinozoisite-(Sr)
Hancockite is now epidote-(Pb)
Tweddillite is now manganipiemontite-(Sr)
Strontiopiemontite is now piemontite-(Sr)
Androsite-(La) is now manganiandrosite-(La)

Because the current concept of the epidote group contains exclusively monoclinic minerals, zoisite, the orthorhombic polymorph of clinozoisite, is no longer a member of the epidote group; however, it is included in this volume because of its close relationship to the group and its importance to collectors.

Table 3 lists some of the discredited, obsolete, or varietal names applied to members of the epidote group.

Table 3. Invalid species and varietal names used for Epidote Minerals

Achmatite	=	epidote
Androsite	=	manganiandrosite-(La), or -(Ce)
Beustite	=	epidote
Escherite	=	epidote
Fouquéite	=	clinozoisite
Hancockite	=	epidote-(Pb)
Lombaardite	=	allanite-(Y)
Magnesium orthite	=	dollaseite-(Ce)
Niigataite	=	clinozoisite-(Sr)
Oisanite	=	epidote
Orthite	=	allanite
Pistacite	=	epidote
Puschkinite	=	epidote
Strontiopiemontite	=	piemontite-(Sr)
Tanzanite	=	blue zoisite
Tawmawite	=	chromian epidote
Thallite	=	epidote
Thulite	=	pink massive zoisite
Tweddillite	=	manganipiemontite-(Sr)
Withamite	=	pleochroic red-yellow manganoan epidote

Formation and Geochemistry

Epidote minerals principally occur as products of regional metamorphism, thermal metamorphism, and during the crystallization of acid igneous rocks. They also occur in hydrothermal deposits (Deer, Howie, and Zussman 1986). They are stable over a very wide range of pressure and temperature, and their wide range of compositions makes them important constituents in many rocks (Franz and Liebscher 2004).

Epidotes are the subject of ongoing research to better understand their formation under various conditions of temperature, pressure, water, and oxygen activity. Experimental studies focusing on the stability of epidote in various model systems, recently summarized by Poli and Schmidt (2004), provide important insights into the processes that occur during metamorphosis.

Studies of microscopic fluid inclusions in epidotes, reviewed by Klemd (2004), contribute to our understanding of hydrothermal fluids that are involved in geologically and economically interesting processes such as geothermal fields, ocean hydrothermal vents, skarn-type ore deposits, and ultra-high pressure metamorphism.

The epidote structure can incorporate significant amounts of Sr, Pb, REE, and actinide elements, as well as many transition metals, as trace elements in the crystal. Large amounts of data have been collected on the distribution of these elements and their partitioning between epidote and magma, hydrothermal fluids, or neighboring mineral phases (Frei et al. 2004).

Epidotes in Igneous Rocks

Epidotes only infrequently crystallize as primary constituents of igneous rocks. They do form in some basic rocks by late recrystallization of pore liquids and are also occasionally found as accessory minerals in some granites (Deer, Howie, and Zussman 1986). Epidote, clinozoisite, and zoisite are found in igneous rocks at several localities in California, including Crestmore, Riverside Co. and in the Pala district, San Diego Co. Allanite is an accessory mineral in pegmatites at Hunter Mt., Inyo Co.; the Kern River uranium area, Kern Co.; with zircon and apatite at Pacoima Canyon, Los Angeles Co.; the Jensen quarry, Riverside Co.; and as inclusions in quartz at the Himalaya mine, San Diego Co. (Pemberton 1983).

Unakites are regarded by some workers as primary igneous rocks produced by crystallization at relatively low temperature in the presence of water. Others attribute the formation of epidote in these rocks to *autometasomatism*, a process in which changes occur during cooling of an igneous mass because of the activity of residual fluids within the mass itself. Still others interpret some unakites as hydrothermally altered basalts or gabbros.

Figure 12. Slab of unakite (epidosite) from Virginia, showing a granitic texture. Compared to the sample from Tennessee shown in Figure 3, this material has relatively more of the pink phase and less of the green epidote; the range of variation seen in unakite offers the lapidary artist great flexibility to select material for a particular color or effect. RJL3184

Epidotes in Metamorphic Rocks

For the working geologist, epidote minerals can be an important indicator of the type and intensity of metamorphism that a deposit has undergone. The term "facies" refers to a rock's general appearance and mineral assemblage, which will depend on both the starting composition and the time-temperature-pressure history of the rock. For example, in the lowest greenschist facies a typical mineral assemblage would be epidote + chlorite + albite + quartz + carbonate. The sorts of reactions that can produce more epidote as the rock is heated include:

(1) chlorite + calcite = epidote + dolomite
(2) chlorite + dolomite = epidote + actinolite

Figure 13. Spherical masses of prehnite with small dark green sprays of epidote crystals filling a pocket about 5 X 9 cm, from Baja California, Mexico. RJL2901

Epidote minerals are fairly common in rocks of blueschist facies and eclogite facies. The transition from greenschist to blueschist is characterized by the relation: actinolite + chlorite + albite = epidote + glaucophane + quartz. The transition from blueschist to eclogite is dominated by the breakdown of lawsonite into epidote minerals (Franz and Liebscher 2004).

For the collector, some types of metamorphic deposits that have produced good-quality specimens include low-grade metamorphic or hydrothermal deposits, contact metamorphic and metasomatic deposits (particularly skarns), and Alpine-cleft type deposits:

Low grade metamorphic assemblages (less than about 300°C) of epidote and prehnite along with chlorite, calcite, and albite can produce outstanding specimens for the collector. Examples of this association are found at Diako, Mali; in Baja California, Mexico; and at the Lane quarry, Westfield, Massachusetts.

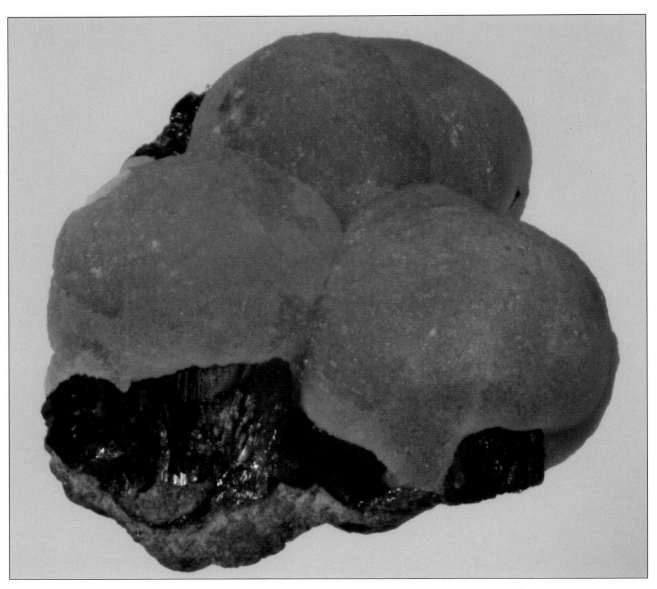

Figure 14. Pale green prehnite in hemispheres about 3 cm in diameter, growing over dark green epidote, from Diako, Mali. This locale has produced a large number of superb specimens in recent years. RJL2761

Epidote is commonly found as a gangue mineral in skarns associated with contact metasomatic ore deposits. Skarns are typically formed at the contact between an igneous intrusion and limestone; epidotes can form in this setting through reactions between the carbonate and oxide minerals and a silica-rich igneous solution. In other instances, chloride-rich solutions may introduce (as $FeCl_3$) the iron needed to form epidote (Franz and Liebscher 2004). Some skarn-type occurrences include Saline Valley, California (epidote with garnet); Prince of Wales Island, Alaska (epidote with quartz); and Traversella, Italy (epidote).

Figure 15. Elongated prismatic epidote on corroded dodecahedral garnets in a typical skarn assemblage from Saline Valley, California. When this material was found, the cavity was likely filled with calcite, which was later etched away with acid to expose the minerals of interest. The small white mass near the bottom of the photo is all that remains of the calcite after specimen preparation. RJL3162

Figure 16. Prince of Wales Island, Alaska, is a classic North American locality for sharp dark green to black epidotes, usually associated with colorless quartz. This specimen is a more unusual combination in which a spherical mass of hematite blades sits on the termination of a large epidote crystal. Specimen is about 4 cm tall. RJL3137

Figure 17. Deep green equant epidote crystals to about 3 cm tall on matrix, from Traversella, Italy. RJL2955

Alpine-cleft deposits develop in small fissures or tension cracks in which a slow-moving hydrothermal fluid infiltrates and recrystallizes the adjacent wall rock. The fluids themselves are thought to be derived from nearby rocks through metamorphic processes. Cleft deposits tend to be small and because the space is confined, removal of specimens is a very painstaking process. A classic European locality of this type is Knappenwand, Austria, where epidote is associated with actinolite var. *byssolite*, albite, calcite, chlorite, diopside, orthoclase var. *adularia*, quartz, and occasionally various metal sulfides. Similar assemblages are found at numerous localities in Piedmont, Italy. At Chamegg Mt., Bern, Switzerland, epidote occurs with actinolite var. *byssolite*, orthoclase var. *adularia*, quartz, pyrrhotite, and scheelite. At its type locale, Bourg d'Oisans, France, epidote is associated with actinolite, albite, manganaxinite, orthoclase, prehnite, and quartz. Occurrences at Khowrin Mt., Markazi Prov., Iran and in the Gamsberg region of Namibia are also cleft-type deposits. The Alpine-cleft deposits of Alchuri, Pakistan have recently produced superb crystals of clinozoisite, epidote, and zoisite, along with numerous other species.

Figure 18. Floater group of sharp, very dark epidote crystals, from Rehoboth, Namibia. RJL3009

Figure 19. Large brown epidote crystals with blades of pale yellow titanite, from Alchuri Pakistan. Specimen is about 8 cm tall. RJL3136

Figure 20. Dark, elongated prismatic epidote crystals, to about 1 cm long, thickly scattered on matrix, from Quam Mts., Iran. RJL3158

The Minerals

A few members of the epidote group (notably clinozoisite-(Sr), mukhinite, and several members of the allanite subgroup) are fairly rare, with only one or a few known localities, whereas others are of worldwide distribution. Most are available to collectors through commercial mineral suppliers.

Clinozoisite subgroup

Clinozoisite was named by Weinschenk in 1896 for its structure and composition as the monoclinic dimorph of zoisite, based on type material from Goslerwand, Pragratten, Tyrol, Austria. It typically forms elongated, often striated, prismatic crystals, but massive, granular, and radial-fibrous forms are also known. The crystals may be colorless or various shades of yellow, green, or pink depending on the amount and type of substitutional impurities. Clinozoisite is a frequent component of regionally metamorphosed rocks (especially greenschist facies) but is also found in some gabbros, pegmatites, and Alpine-cleft type deposits. It also occurs in acid igneous rocks contaminated with calc-silicates. It has been documented from hundreds of localities worldwide; the following may be of particular interest to collectors: At Alamos, Sonora, Mexico bright pink to greenish acicular crystals and spherical aggregates are associated with massive quartz. Pink to tan elongated crystals to several cm long are found near Taylorsville, California. Extremely large, sharp, gemmy crystals are found at Hashupa and at Alchuri, in the Shigar Valley, Northern Areas, Pakistan (Blauwet 2006). Good crystals are found in Alpine-type deposits near Zermatt, Switzerland and in the Italian Alps. Green crystals to several cm long are associated with actinolite var. *byssolite* and numerous other species in amphibolite gneiss at the Keystone trap rock quarry, Cornog, Pennsylvania. Pink to green crystals in large sprays are found in a pegmatite at Volondandrongo, Madagascar. Pale tan to golden crystals in radiating clusters are reported from several localities in Peru.

Clinozoisite-(Sr) was originally named *niigataite* for the type locale, in the Itoigawa-Ohmi district, Niigata Prefecture, in central Japan (Miyajima et al. 2003). It was found in a boulder of prehnite rock in which the prehnite formed typical fan-shaped aggregates. Interstitially within the prehnite, the type material consisted of minute pale gray grains intimately intergrown with chlorite and diaspore, and closely associated with strontian clinozoisite (i.e., clinozoisite that contains some Sr but not enough for Sr to occupy more than half of the **A2** sites). Clinozoisite-(Sr) has also been found in a sample of pumpellyite rock from the Wakasa district, Tottori Prefecture, Japan. The host rock consisted of very fine grains of pumpellyite, chlorite, clinozoisite, and jadeite. Microscopic analysis showed that clinozoisite-(Sr) rims (**A2** $\sim$ $Sr_{0.8}Ca_{0.2}$) surrounded strontian clinozoisite cores (**A2** $\sim$ $Ca_{0.9}Sr_{0.1}$).

Figure 21. Radiating, pale yellow/tan clinozoisite crystals, from Huatara, Peru. RJL2769

Figure 22. Another cluster of tan clinozoisite crystals from Huancavelica, Peru. Interestingly, this specimen was identified by the seller as zoisite, but XRD analysis confirmed that this specimen and the one in the previous figure are both clinozoisite. Other than the size of the crystals, the two samples are very similar and one has to wonder if perhaps they came from the same place. RJL2935

Figure 23. Pink acicular clinozoisite forming radiating masses, from Alamos, Sonora, Mexico. RJL2900

Figure 24. Sharp tabular clinozoisite crystal about 2 cm tall on colorless quartz, from Hashupa, Shigar Valley, Pakistan. RJL2979

Figure 25. Flattened clinozoisite crystals 6 cm tall, from Hashupa, Pakistan. Both the large crystal and the smaller one have significant bends in several directions, which healed as the crystals continued to grow. RJL3033

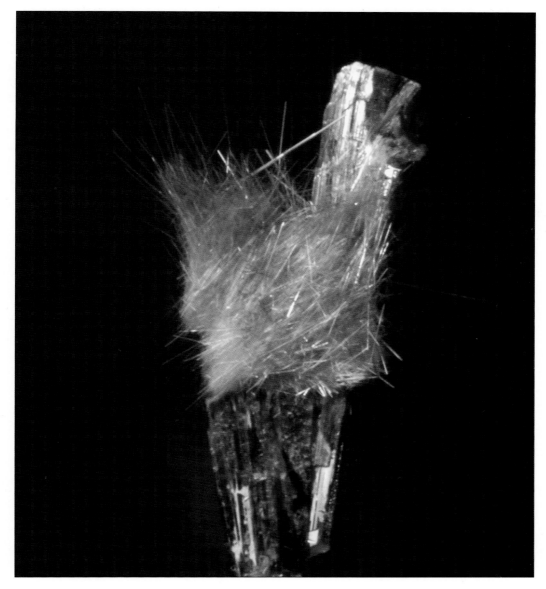

Figure 26. Dull brownish clinozoisite crystal about 4 cm tall, with hair-like actinolite var. *byssolite* from the Keystone trap rock quarry, Cornog, Pennsylvania. RJL2937

Figure 27. Tan, bladed clinozoisite crystals to several cm in matrix from near Taylorsville, Plumas Co., California. RJL3013

Epidote was described in 1801 by Haüy, who derived the name from the Greek word for "increase" because the base of the rhombohedral prism has one side larger than the other. The obsolete name *pistacite* alludes to its characteristic pistachio-green color. Epidote is the best known and perhaps most widely distributed mineral in the group, with thousands of documented localities worldwide. It is "a ubiquitous mineral in regional and contact-metamorphic rocks" and also occurs in metasomatic skarns, epithermal ore deposits, low-temperature veins, and in granites and pegmatites (Gaines et al. 1997). Recognizing that it is difficult to do justice to the breadth and quality of epidote locales, the following occurrences certainly merit the interest of collectors: Within the U.S., the Green Monster mine, Prince of Wales Island, Alaska has yielded superb specimens of lustrous prismatic crystals with quartz (Leavens and Thomssen 1997); the Calumet iron mine, Chaffee County, Colorado is a notable locale for simple striated euhedral crystals. Large bladed crystals forming dark fans with quartz are found at Pampa Blanca, Huancavelica, Peru. Striated elongated prismatic crystals in groups, alone or with colorless quartz, white albite, or more rarely, yellow-green titanite, from the Fazenda Rubin Pimenta mine, Capelinha, Minas Gerais, Brazil are relatively inexpensive and plentiful at present. Extremely sharp, lustrous crystals are found at Knappenwand, Untersulzbachtal, Austria associated with gray-green fibrous *byssolite*. Fine green to black crystals are found in skarn at Traversella, Piedmont, Italy. Epidote "gwindels" form attractive floater groups at Pamir, Tadzhikistan. Similar stacked groups are found in Pakistan. Also from Pakistan, brilliant lustrous black sheaf-like groups to 3 cm tall with colorless quartz are found at Wadd, Baluchistan; stubby crystals with milky quartz are found in the Kharan Mountains. Recently, superb specimens of epidote with quartz from Sichuan Prov., China have been plentiful. These are noteworthy because of the wide variety of aesthetic combinations, which range from isolated olive-green epidotes perched on large colorless quartz crystals to solid plates of epidote with quartz as an accessory. Adding to the interest, the quartz crystals occasionally have colorful phantoms or inclusions of hematite or other species. Lustrous aggregates with colorless quartz have also become available from Rigma, Midelt, Morocco. Sharp, dark crystals with green botryoidal prehnite from Diako, Mali have become very well known in the past few years and are destined to become a "classic" occurrence. Many other locales for good epidote specimens are mentioned in a recent review (Cook 2002).

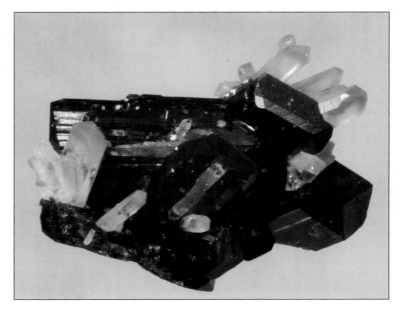

Figure 28. A classic combination: equant, dark green epidote crystals with colorless quartz, from Green Monster claim, Prince of Wales Is., Alaska. RJL2797

Figure 29. Lustrous, striated epidotes in matrix, from the Calumet iron mine, Colorado. RJL2956

Figure 30. A very large specimen showing bladed epidote crystals to 6 cm long in radiating clusters associated with color-less quartz crystals to 16 cm long, from Pampa Blanca, Peru. Specimen is 25 cm wide at the base. RJL2959

Figure 31. Elongated prismatic epidotes with colorless quartz, from the Fazenda Rubin Pimenta mine, Capelhina, Brazil. Material of this type is relatively plentiful at present. RJL2858

Figure 32. A less-common association from the Fazenda Rubin Pimenta mine, Capelhina, Brazil: dark green epidotes with greenish yellow titanite crystals. RJL2798

Figure 33. Dark green prismatic epidote crystals, each about 1 cm long, on colorless quartz from Salzburg, Austria. RJL2856

Figure 34. Olive-green euhedral epidote crystals from the Piedmont Region, Italy. RJL2875

Figure 35. A thumbnail-sized specimen of epidote with hair-like fibers of actinolite var. *byssolite* from the classic locality at Knappenwand, Austria. RJL2506

Figure 36. A milky quartz crystal about 5 cm tall on a bed of greenish-black elongated epidotes in subparallel clusters, from the Kharan Mts., Pakistan. RJL2786

Figure 37. Milky quartz intergrown with small green epidotes, from Johnson Hill, California. RJL2953

Figure 38. Lustrous, subparallel sprays of epidote with colorless quartz, from Wadd, Pakistan. RJL3034

Figure 39. An epidote gwindel from Pakistan. The darker bands of color on the lower part of the specimen appear to be inclusions of actinolite or possibly aegirine. RJL2787

Figure 40. A fine, dark epidote gwindel from Pamir, Tadjikistan. Doubly-terminated individuals are progressively rotated about 20° in their common plane, with a second set of crystals interpenetrating them. RJL1680

Figure 41. A large, colorless quartz crystal, about 10 cm tall, associated with sprays of green epidote, from the Honqizhen quarry, China. RJL3159

Figure 42. A solid plate of pistachio-green epidote with colorless quartz, from Sichuan Province, China. Specimen is about 12 cm wide. RJL2958

Figure 43. A fine spray of lustrous epidote crystals, from Ica, Peru. RJL1853

Figure 44. Small, rich green epidote crystals on a plate of heavily included quartz from Sichuan Province, China. RJL2928

Figure 45. Detail of specimen in Figure 44 showing a colorful association of pistachio-green epidote and clear quartz with red and white inclusions. This sample, along with that in Figure 42, shows some of the diversity of fine Chinese epidote specimens that are plentiful at present. RJL2928

Figure 46. Clusters of small, lustrous green epidote with drusy quartz, from Midelt, Morocco. RJL2725

Figure 47. Moss-like sprays of epidote with quartz from Alicante, Spain. This specimen clearly illustrates the distinctive color to which the name "pistacite" refers. RJL2952

Figure 48. An interesting association: green epidote with gray-brown bladed crystals of ferroaxinite, from Huancavelica, Peru. RJL2193

Figure 49. Spray of prismatic dark green epidote from San Quinton, Baja California, Mexico. Note the similarity to some of the material from Peru. RJL2954

Figure 50. An excellent example of manganoan epidote that is deep red but does not meet the compositional specification for piemontite. This mass of brilliant red acicular crystals is from Jebel Shagro, Morocco. RJL3087

Figure 51. Another interesting association: a brown, prismatic epidote crystal 4 cm tall, perched on a chlorite-coated orthoclase var. *adularia* crystal, from Alchuri, Pakistan. RJL3135

Figure 52. Epidote on prehnite from Baja California, Mexico: detail of specimen in Figure 13, showing clusters of small dark green epidote crystals thickly scattered among white to pale greenish spherical aggregates of prehnite. RJL2901

Figure 53. Another example of epidote associated with spherical prehnite aggregates: this specimen, about 2 X 4 cm, is from Bull Run quarry, Virginia. RJL3125

Epidote-(Pb) was originally described as *hancockite* in 1899 by S. L. Penfield and C. H. Warren as one of a handful of new minerals from the Parker Shaft, Franklin, New Jersey (Palache 1935). The small, lathlike crystals are generally under 1 mm but can be as large as 2 cm. Color is usually some shade of red to brown, occasionally yellowish-brown to yellow-green. At the type locale it is associated with garnet, hendricksite, datolite, and manganaxinite in fractures in willemite-franklinite ore. It has also been found in a metamorphosed manganese-iron orebody in skarns at Jakobsberg, Varmland, Sweden.

Figure 54. Brown, microcrystalline epidote-(Pb), formerly known as *hancockite*, from the Parker shaft, Franklin, New Jersey. RJL3014

IMA2006-055 describes compositions analogous to clinozoisite-(Sr) but with Fe^{3+} as the dominant ion on **M3**. As of this writing, formal description of the species and the type locale is pending; a "recommended" name was listed in the official guidelines established for the group (Armbruster et al. 2006) but an official name will only be accepted when the description is published. Meanwhile, in addition to the type material, samples falling within this compositional field have also been recognized at the Wessels mine, South Africa. Identification of the phase at Wessels was done by Dr. Nikita Chukanov using electron microprobe, X-ray powder diffraction, and IR spectroscopy data (N. V. Chukanov, personal communication). At Wessels, the material is red, presumably due to the presence of some Mn [compare manganipiemontite-(Sr)].

Mukhinite is thus far the only V-dominant member of the clinozoisite subgroup. It was described from material in a borehole at the Tashelginskoe iron deposit, near the mouth of the Tashelga River, Gornaya Shoria, in the Kemerovo district of southwest Siberia, Russia (Shepel' and Karpenko 1969). The species forms small black crystals (1 x 2.5 mm and aggregates to 5 mm) in marble, associated with goldmanite, muscovite, pyrite, pyrrhotite, sphalerite, and galena. It has also been noted from skarns at Kuznetsk in southern Kazakhstan associated with garnet, diopside, clinozoisite, titanite, galena, and quartz. In the U.S., mukhinite is reported from Lewistown, Montana.

Figure 55. Brilliant red needles of the Fe-dominant analogue of clinozoisite-(Sr) forming a solid mass, from the Wessels mine, South Africa. The red color is caused by traces of manganese. RJL3127

Piemontite is the manganese analogue of clinozoisite, with Mn^{3+} substituting for Al at the **M3** site. Historically the name was applied rather indiscriminately to any manganiferous epidotes showing strong red-yellow-violet pleochroism. A recent study (Bonazzi and Menchetti 2004) reviewed the chemistry and structure of piemontite and its related minerals and discussed its paragenesis at dozens of localities worldwide. It was seen early on that the mineral is not found in many Mn-rich deposits where it might be expected. This riddle is best understood by reference to Table 2 where it can be seen that all of the piemontites contain *trivalent* Mn on the **M3** site. Thus, the mineral can only form where there is sufficient manganese and the conditions are sufficiently oxidizing to create Mn^{3+}. At the type locale, the Praborna manganese mine, St. Marcel, Val D'Aosta, Italy piemontite forms deep red bladed crystals and masses in the upper zone of a metamorphic manganese ore deposit. This material reportedly has significant amounts of Sr substituting for Ca. At the Cassagna mine, Val Greveglia, Italy it is found as well-formed crystals to 3 mm with pyrolusite and quartz (Marchesini and Pagano 2001). Rough deep red crystals are found near Pilar, New Mexico. Dense veins of radiating acicular crystals are found in metarhyolite on Culp Ridge, Iron Springs, Pennsylvania. In Japan, piemontite schist is found in the Sonoki and Sangun metamorphic zones; it is also found as 3-cm acicular crystals at Otakiyama, Tokushima Pref., and as crystals with braunite at the Tone mine, Nagasaki Pref. Translucent to transparent crystals to 6 mm are found with colorless quartz in the Messina mines, South Africa.

Figure 56. Deep red laths of piemontite from the type locale, the Praborna mine, Italy. RJL3015

Figure 57. Detail of the piemontite specimen shown in Figure 56. RJL3015

Figure 58. Small, brick red mass of piemontite in quartz, from Pilar, New Mexico. RJL2988

Figure 59. Deep red needles of piemontite in radiating masses, from a classic American locale, Culp Ridge, Pennsylvania. RJL3060

Figure 60. Detail of the piemontite specimen shown in Figure 59. RJL3060

Figure 61. Small red needles of piemontite in massive quartz, from Washoe Co., Nevada. RJL3142

Piemontite-(Sr), originally described as *strontiopiemontite*, differs from piemontite by the substitution of Sr for Ca at the **A2** site. It was first found at the Cassagna and Molinello mines, Val Graveglia, Liguria, Italy as small dark red veins and elongated prismatic crystals associated with quartz, calcite, rhodochrosite, rhodonite, and ganophyllite (Bonazzi, Menchetti, and Palenzona 1990). It also occurs at the Praborna manganese mine, St. Marcel, Val d'Aosta, Piedmont, Italy. Small crystals and larger masses are found with pectolite at the Wessels mine, South Africa. Also reported from low-grade manganese ore in metamorphosed sediments at Shiromaru mine, Okutama, Japan.

Manganipiemontite-(Sr) was originally described as *tweddillite* from the Wessels mine, Kalahari manganese field, South Africa (Armbruster et al. 2002) where it occurs in calcsilicate rocks formed by hydrothermal alteration (250 to 400°C) of primary sedimentary manganese ore. The mineral forms dark red radiating aggregates of minute, thin-bladed crystals (~0.02 mm thick and up to 0.5 mm long) associated with serandite, pectolite, and braunite. Similar material has been reported from the Sanbagawa metamorphic belt, central Shikoku, Japan, where it occurs in a piemontite quartzose schist associated with braunite and hollandite.

Figure 62. Thin layer of glassy red microcrystalline piemontite-(Sr) on matrix from the type locale, the Cassagna mine, Val Graveglia, Italy. RJL3016

Allanite subgroup

Allanite was named for the Scottish mineralogist Thomas Allan (1777-1833) based on type material from Greenland [see Peterson, Secher and Bich (2006) for historical background.] Under modern nomenclature, that material is allanite-(Ce). Later workers described additional compositions that are now denoted allanite-(La) and allanite-(Y). Allanites are a common accessory mineral in granite, granodiorite, monzonite, syenite, and granitic pegmatite. They are also found in diorite and gabbro, as phenocrysts in acid volcanic rocks, and in a number of metamorphic rock types.

Many allanites contain uranium and thorium in addition to rare earth elements. According to the literature reviewed by Gieré and Sorensen (2004), the maximum reported ThO_2 content is 4.9 wt.% which would correspond to about 0.07 Th atoms per formula unit (apfu). The maximum UO_2 content is 0.82 wt.% in a crystal that also contained 1.09 wt.% ThO_2, corresponding to 0.02 apfu of each. Thus, the actinide (ACT) elements Th and U are relatively minor constituents in these minerals, and for classification purposes the sum of ACT and REE is used. The recommended chemical criterion to assign minerals to the allanite and dollaseite subgroups is REE + ACT > 0.5 apfu. The justification for bundling U and Th with REE is that the coupled heterovalent substitution mechanism is presumably: $^{A2}(Th^{4+}, U^{4+}) + 2\ ^{M3}M^{2+}$ → $^{A2}Ca + 2\ ^{M3}M^{3+}$.

The presence of radioactive elements brings up another complication: many REE-bearing epidote minerals are partly or completely metamict. One traditional approach to studying metamict minerals is to anneal the sample in order to re-crystallize or "heal" the radiation damage and thereby restore the crystal structure for X-ray analysis. The problem is that a metamict mineral is fairly reactive and may adsorb soluble elements from the environment or undergo ion exchange. Thus, the "restored" crystal might have a composition that differs significantly from that of the original crystal and in effect becomes a synthetic material. As stated by Armbruster et al. (2006): "There is at least some suspicion that such 'mineral' compositions are influenced by the experimenter and are not an unaltered product of nature. These problems are not specific of epidote-group minerals but are much more prominent in other mineral groups with higher concentrations of radioisotopes. ... We recommend exercising caution with compositions of 'partly' metamict epidote-group minerals in naming new species, even if the 'faulty' lattice has been mended by subsequent heat treatment."

It is appropriate to mention here that *contact allanite deposits* are an interesting class of uranium ore resources. These deposits occur in contact zones between intrusives and various sedimentary rocks. In some of these occurrences allanite and other REE minerals are abundant but only weakly radioactive, whereas in others the allanite is responsible for considerable radioactivity. Deposits of this type include the Whalen mine in west-central Alaska; Grand Calumet Is., Quebec, Canada; the Kyshtymsk district, Ural Mts., Russia; and at Bastnaes and at the Östanmossa mine, Sweden. At the Mary Kathleen deposit, Queensland, Australia, the allanite itself is not radioactive, but disseminated grains of uraninite are present and in the oxidized zone uranophane, uranophane-ß, and *gummite* are found (Heinrich 1958).

Allanite-(Ce) was first described from Qaparssuatsiaq, Aluk, South Greenland, and has since been documented from nearly 300 localities worldwide. Especially large crystals (some well over a foot long) have been found at the Rutherford mine, Amelia, Virginia. Sharp, tabular crystals are found at the Tiro Estrella mine, Lincoln County, New Mexico in quartz veins with feldspar. At the Trimouns talc deposit, Ariege, France, fine crystals and sprays up to 2 cm are found in dolomite, often associated with other REE-bearing species (Marty 2004). Some other locales include: Copper Gulch, Fremont County, Colorado; Pacoima Canyon, Los Angeles County, California; in the vicinity of Bancroft, Ontario, Canada; Arendal, Norway; Finnbo, Sweden; and Clarte, Cotes-du-Nord, France.

Figure 63. Tabular black allanite-(Ce) crystals to about 5 mm long, from the Tiro Estrella mine, New Mexico. RJL3012

Figure 64. An interesting association: a cluster of sharp, transparent orange, tabular bastnäsite-(Ce) crystals perched on elongated, brownish green allanite-(Ce) from the Trimouns mine, Ariege, France. Sample is about 2 cm tall. RJL2800

Figure 65. Dark brown, striated allanite-(Ce) crystal about 15 mm long, on pearly yellow dolomite, from the Trimouns mine, Ariege, France. RJL3064

Figure 66. Crude tabular crystal of allanite-(Ce) about 4 X 5 cm, from Oso Township, Ontario, Canada. RJL2638

Figure 67. Black tabular allanite-(Ce) crystals forming a thumbnail-sized cluster, from Torghar, Pakistan. RJL3035

Allanite-(La) denotes those compositions where La is the dominant REE element. Allanites that meet this definition had been known for some time, but to formalize the name allanite-(La) was recently described as a "new" mineral from the Buca della Vena mine, near Stazzema, Tuscany, Italy (Orlando and Pasero 2006). At the type locale it forms black prismatic crystals 2-3 mm long in barite veins cutting a dolomitic metamorphosed limestone. It is known from over a dozen localities, making it rather rare compared to allanite-(Ce). The finest specimens of allanite-(La) were found at the Nueva Vizcaya mine, Badajoz, Spain, where sharp crystals as large as 4 cm occur in an Fe-Ca skarn. Associated minerals include magnetite, actinolite, albite, epidote, and titanite (Gonzales del Tanago and Graf 2002). Other occurrences include: the Hemlo gold mine, Thunder Bay district, Ontario, Canada; in a diorite cut by pegmatite veins at the Stahl quarry, Bavaria, Germany; at several pumice quarries near Niedermendig, Laach Lake volcanic complex, Rhineland-Palatinate, Germany; in a quartz monzonite pluton at Mt. Falconer, South Victoria Land, Antarctica; Wilmot Pass, South Island, New Zealand; the Jones Mill quarry, Magnet Cove, Arkansas; in pegmatite at Baringer Hill, Bluffton, Texas; and Ragged Peak, Yosemite National Park, California.

Allanite-(Y) was originally described as *lombaardite* from the Zaaiplaats tin mine, Transvaal, South Africa. Later work suggested that *lombaardite* is identical to a Y_2O_3-dominant allanite from Askagen, Värmland, Sweden, which is now considered to be the type locale (Armbruster et al. 2006). Well-crystallized micro material is found at the Marble quarries, Kilchrist, Isle of Skye, Scotland. Other localities include: in pegmatite at

the Gole quarry, Madawaska, Ontario, Canada; in a nepheline-albite pegmatite at the Davis quarry, Bancroft district, Ontario, Canada; in a yttrium-bearing pegmatite at Suishoyama, Kawamata, Fukushima Pref., Japan; the Tanger feldspar quarry, Telemark, Norway associated with other Y- and REE-bearing species; several quarries at Mount Camoscio, Piedmont, Italy; and Boden, in the Erzgebirge, Saxony, Germany.

Figure 68. Sharp black prismatic crystal of allanite-(La) about 8 mm tall, on greenish hedenbergite, from the Nueva Vizcaya mine, Badajoz, Spain. RJL3007

Ferriallanite-(Ce) is the analogue of allanite-(Ce) with Fe^{3+} dominant on the **M3** site. It was described from a metasomatic deposit in the Neprimetnyi alkaline granitic pegmatite on the northern slope of Mount Ulyn Khuren, which is part of the Khaldzan Buragtag peralkaline granite massif, Mongolia. It forms small (up to about 1 mm) black, subhedral grains in masses of zircon, quartz, and kainosite-(Y). Associated minerals include aegirine, ilvaite, magnetite, fayalite, fluorite, and several REE-containing species (Kartashov et al. 2002). Other occurrences include: a carbonatite vein at the Biraya Fe-REE orebody, Transbaikalia, Russia; in carbonate rocks altered by alkaline metasomatism in the Chergilen rare-earth occurrence, Chekunda, Khabarovskiy Kray, Russia; with other REE species in a gold placer at Kyshtym, Chelyabinsk, Russia; in a metasomatic Zr-REE-Nb deposit at Chungju, South Korea; and at the noted REE deposit at Bastnäs mines, Västmanland, Sweden.

Dissakisite-(Ce) is the magnesium analogue of allanite-(Ce), i.e., Mg replaces Fe^{2+} on the **M3** site. It was first described from marble on Balchen Mountain, East Antarctica in association with calcite, dolomite, forsterite, clinohumite, phlogopite, *chlorite*, spinel, zircon, and other species (Grew et al. 1991). The mineral forms minute (0.05 – 0.6 mm) brown-yellow grains at the interfaces between the other mineral phases present in the marble. At the type locale it is believed to have formed under metamorphic conditions at about 600°C. The mineral has also been reported from a tremolite skarn at Östanmossa, Sweden, as well as in the Aldan Shield, southern Yakutia, Russia, where it occurs in diopside-phlogopite rocks (magnesian skarns) at the Fedorovskoye and Emel'dzhak deposits. Chromian dissakisite has been reported from the Outokumpu mining district, Finland associated with chromian phlogopite and a Zn-Cr rich spinel. For collectors, the most readily available dissakisite-(Ce) comes from the Trimouns talc deposit, France, in the form of elongated to lathlike crystals on dolomite.

Dissakisite-(La), the Mg analogue of allanite-(La), was first described from the Hochwart peridotite, Ulten zone, Italy, where it forms black to very dark brown cm-sized anhedral nodules and smaller grains. Associated minerals include olivine, spinel, pyroxenes and amphiboles, uraninite, thorite, thorianite, and numerous others (Tumiati et al. 2005; Tumiati et al. 2006). It is also reported from a gold placer at Kyshtym, Chelyabinsk, Russia, where it occurs with bastnäsite-(La) and other REE species.

Figure 69. Pale brown dissakisite-(Ce) crystal, about 6 mm tall, on dolomite from the Trimouns mine, Ariege, France. RJL3025

Manganiandrosite-(La) was originally described as androsite-(La) from samples collected on the heap of a former manganese ore test pit on Petalon Mountain, Andros Island, Greece. The ore is made up of highly oxidized schists, quartzites, and Mn-rich pyroxenoid and carbonate rocks. In the Mn-rich silicate-carbonate rock, manganiandrosite-(La) forms minute brown-red grains (typically 20-60 μm) randomly dispersed in a fine-grained matrix of rhodonite, rhodochrosite, braunite, and spessartine (Bonazzi, Menchetti, and Reinecke 1996). It is also noted at the Chudnoe Pd-Au deposit, Grubependity Lake, Komi Republic, Russia.

Figure 70. Photomicrograph of red-brown manganiandrosite-(La) from Chudnoe Pd-Au deposit, Grubependity Lake, Komi Republic, Russia. Field of view is about 5 mm wide. RJL3211

Manganiandrosite-(Ce) has been found in metamorphosed manganese-bearing sediments from the Praborna manganese mine, St. Marcel, Italy, associated with rhodochrosite, Mn-pyroxenoid, spessartine, hematite, calderite, and pyrophanite. The crystals are pleochroic, light yellow, orange-brown, and red-brown (Chopin et al. 2006; Cenki-Tok et al. 2006).

Vanadoandrosite-(Ce) is defined by dominant V^{3+} at the **M1** site. It is found in the Vielle Aure mining district, central Pyrenees, France in quartz-rhodochrosite-sulfide veinlets cutting rhodochrosite ore in Lower Carboniferous radiolarite. The crystals are pleochroic, yellow brown, red-brown, and dark greenish brown. Associated minerals include vuorelainenite, chalcopyrite, vanadian spessartine, and friedelite (Chopin et al. 2006; Cenki-Tok et al. 2006).

Dollaseite subgroup

Dollaseite-(Ce) was originally described as "magnesium orthite" by Geijer in 1927, based on material from the Östanmossa mine, Norberg district, Sweden. At the time the mineral was thought to be simply the Mg analogue of allanite ("orthite"). Later analytical work determined that its composition corresponds to the site occupancies shown in Table 2, with Mg on both **M1** and **M3** sites and charge compensation achieved by substitution of F⁻ for O^{2-} on the **O4** site. At the type locale dollaseite-(Ce) forms massive brown aggregates of sub-mm crystals associated with tremolite, norbergite, and calcite. It is also reported from several mines in the Moklinta ore field, Avesta, Sweden.

Khristovite-(Ce) was first described from a rhodonite occurrence in the Muzeinyi Sai ("Museum Valley"), Trudovoye tin deposit, on the northern slope of the Inyl'chek Range, eastern Kyrgyzstan. It forms dark brown grains and prismatic crystals to 1.5 mm associated with rhodonite, tephroite, spessartine, and various other manganese and tin minerals and base metal sulfides (Pautov et al. 1993)

Related species

Zoisite, the orthorhombic polymorph of clinozoisite, was described by Werner in 1805 based on material from the Sau Alpe Mts., Carinthia, Austria. Zoisites have a fairly limited range of compositions: replacement of Al by Fe^{3+} is usually less than about 10% so there is no solid solution series extending to an orthorhombic analogue of epidote. Similarly, the manganese responsible for the pink color of *thulite* is present in relatively small amounts, so there is no orthorhombic analogue of piemontite. Zoisite is fairly common in regionally metamorphosed calcarious shales and sandstones, and in amphibolites resulting from the regional metamorphosis of basic igneous rocks. It is also occasionally found in low-grade thermally metamorphosed impure limestones and skarns. Hydrothermal alteration of calcium-rich plagioclase (a process referred to as *sassuritization*) can also form zoisite.

Among the hundreds of documented localities, the following are of particular interest to collectors. In the Arusha district of Tanzania, transparent euhedral crystals in various shades of brown, blue, yellow, pink, or greenish are found in the Merelani Hills, and massive green zoisite var. *anyolite* is found at Longido. Pink massive zoisite var. *thulite* was mined at several locales in Norway, including: Sauland, Telemark; Hidrum, Trondelag; and Lom, Oppland. Green columnar crystals are found at Gandegg, Switzerland. Excellent elongated prismatic crystals are found at several localities in the Northern Areas, Pakistan: at Alchuri, Shigar Valley, Skardu district (colorless to green crystals); and at Turmiq, northwest of Skardu (colorless to grayish crystals).

Figure 71. Massive green zoisite var. *anyolite* with black amphibole grains from Merkerstein, Tanzania. RJL3017

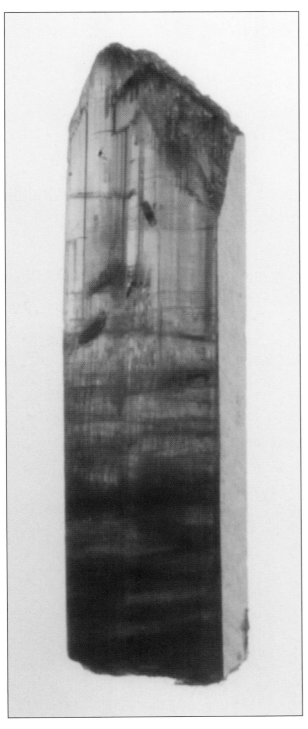

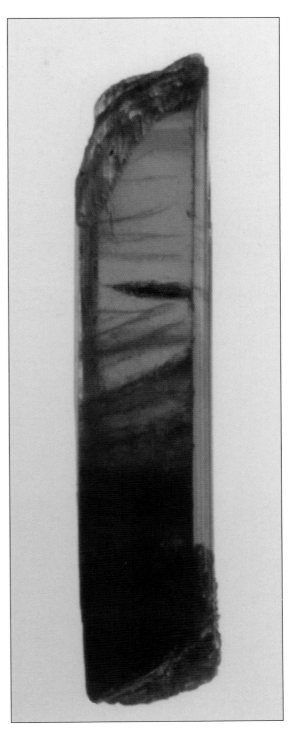

Figure 72. Transparent green zoisite crystal about 3 cm tall, from Tanzania. RJL1468

Figure 73. The same zoisite crystal as in the previous photo, rotated 90 degrees to demonstrate its pronounced pleochroism. RJL1468

Figure 74. Large, transparent, nearly colorless zoisite crystals on skarn from Shigar, Pakistan. Largest crystal is about 25 mm tall. RJL3124.

Figure 75. Colorless, terminated zoisite crystals about 15 mm tall on dolomite, from an occurrence near Alchuri, Pakistan. RJL2993

Figure 76. Large, dark, greenish-brown zoisite crystal about 8 cm tall, from Alchuri, Pakistan. RJL2978

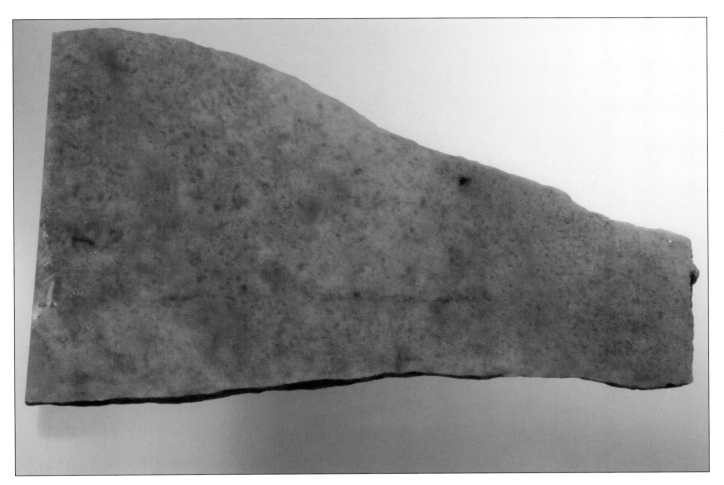

Figure 77. Slab of zoisite var. *thulite* from eastern Washington. This material would make excellent subtle pink cabochons. RJL3182

Figure 78. Pink needles of zoisite on a thin plate of muscovite about 10 cm wide, from Micaville, North Carolina. RJL2994

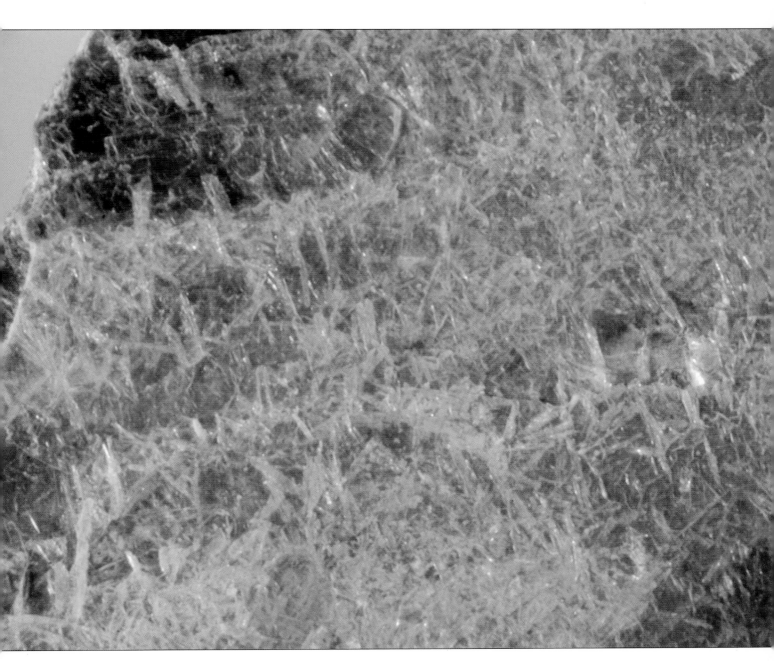

Figure 79. Detail of specimen in the previous figure, showing interlocking zoisite crystals forming a thin crust on the surface of the mica. RJL2994

Bibliography

In addition to the references cited, readers interested in a comprehensive scientific review of the epidote group might consider the book, *Epidotes, Reviews in Mineralogy and Geochemistry* Vol. 56, Axel Liebscher and Gerhard Franz, editors, available from the Mineralogical Society of America (2004). This volume of review papers, citing thousands of original references and reports, clearly shows the complexity of the epidote group and its importance to the science of petrology and geochemistry.

Readers can find an excellent on-line searchable mineral and locality database at www.mindat.org, which provides an extensive locality listing for each mineral, as well as other useful information for collectors and mineralogists. Users are cautioned, however, that individual entries on that web site (and many others) are not peer-reviewed, and unless an actual reference is cited, locality information should be regarded as tentative.

Armbruster, T., P. Bonazzi, M. Akasaka, V. Bermanec, C. Chopin, R. Giere, S. Heuss-Assbichler, A. Liebscher, S. Menchetti, Y. Pan, and M. Pasero 2006. Recommended nomenclature of epidote-group minerals, *European Journal of Mineralogy*, 18: 551-67.

Armbruster, T., E. Gnos, R. Dixon, J. Gutzmer, C. Hejny, N. Dobelin, and O. Medenbach, O. 2002. Manganvesuvianite and tweddillite, two new Mn^{3+}-silicate minerals from Kalahari manganese fields, South Africa, *Mineralogical Magazine* 66 (1): 137-50.

Blauwet, D. 2006. Famous mineral localities: Alchuri, Shigar Valley, Northern Areas, Pakistan, *Mineralogical Record* 37 (6): 513-40.

Bonazzi, P., and S. Menchetti 2004. Manganese in monoclinic members of the epidote group: piemontite and related minerals, *Reviews in Mineralogy and Geochemistry* 46: 495-552.

Bonazzi, P., S. Menchetti, and A. Palenzona 1990. Strontiopiemontite, a new member of the epidote group from Val Graveglia, *European Journal of Mineralogy*, 46: 519-23.

Bonazzi, P., S. Menchetti, and T. Reinecke 1996. Solid solution between piemontite and androsite-(La), a new mineral of the epidote group from Andros Island, Greece, *American Mineralogist*, 81: 735-42.

Cenki-Tok, B., A. Ragu, T. Armbruster, C. Chopin, and O. Medenbach 2006. New Mn- and rare-earth-rich epidote-group minerals in metacherts: androsite-(Ce) and vanadoandrosite-(Ce), *European Journal of Mineralogy* 18: 551-67.

Chopin, C., T. Armbruster, B. Cenki-Tok, and A. Ragu, A. 2006. REE-bearing epidotes in Mn-rich systems: new compounds and fO$_2$ controls, *Geophysical Research Abstracts*, Vol. 8, 08063.

Cook, R. B 2002. Epidote: Knappenwand, Unter-sulzbachtal, Salzburg, Austria – Connoisseur's Choice, *Rocks & Minerals* 77 (5): 328-32.

Deer, W. A., R. A. Howie, and J. Zussman 1986. *Rock-Forming Minerals*, Vol. 1B Disilicates and Ring Silicates, London: Longman's.

Franz, G., and A. Liebscher 2004. Physical and chemical properties of the epidote minerals – An introduction, *Reviews in Mineralogy and Geochemistry* 56: 1-81.

Frei, D., A. Liebscher, G. Franz, and P. Dulski 2004. Trace element geochemistry in epidote minerals, *Reviews in Mineralogy and Geochemistry* 56: 553-605.

Gaines, R.V., H. C. W. Skinner, E. E. Foord, B. Mason, and A. Rosenzweig 1997. *Dana's New Mineralogy*, Eighth Edition, New York: Wiley.

Giere, R., and S. Sorensen 2004. Allanite and other REE-rich epidote-group minerals, *Reviews in Mineralogy and Geochemistry* 56: 431-93.

Goldschmidt, V. 1916. *Atlas der Krystallformen* [see Facsimile Reprint in Nine Volumes (1986) by the Rochester Mineralogical Symposium].

Gonzales del Tanago, J., and B. Graf 2002. The Nueva Vizcaya Mine, Burguilles Del Cerro, Badajoz, Spain, *Mineralogical Record* 33 (6): 489-500.

Grew, E. S., E. J. Essene, D. R. Peacor, S.-C. Su, and M. Asami 1991. Dissakisite-(Ce), a new member of the epidote group and the Mg analogue of allanite-(Ce), from Antarctica, *American Mineralogist* 76: 1990-7.

Heinrich, E. 1958. *Mineralogy and Geology of Radioactive Raw Materials*, New York: McGraw-Hill.

Kartashov, P., G. Ferraris, G. Ivaldi, E. Sokolova, and C. McCammon 2002. Ferriallanite, a new member of the epidote group: description, X-ray, and Mossbauer study, *Canadian Mineralogist* 40: 1641-8.

Keller, P. 1992. *Gemstones of East Africa,* Phoenix: Geoscience Press.

Klemd, R. 2004. Fluid inclusions in epidote minerals and fluid development in epidote-bearing rocks, *Reviews in Mineralogy and Geochemistry* 56: 197-234.

Leavens, P., and R. Thomssen 1977. Famous mineral localities: Prince of Wales Island, Alaska, *Mineralogical Record* 8 (1): 4-12.

Marchesini, M., and R. Pagano 2001. The Val Graveglia manganese district, Liguria, Italy, *Mineralogical Record* 32 (5): 349-415.

Marty, F. 2004. The Trimouns quarry, Luzenac, Ariege, France, *Mineralogical Record* 35 (3): 225-74.

Miyajima, H., S. Matsubara, R. Miyawaki and K. Hirokawa 2003. Niigataite: Sr-analogue of clinozoisite, a new member of the epidote group from the Itoigawa-Ohmi district, Niigata Prefecture, central Japan, *Journal of Mineralogical and Petrological Science* 98: 118-29 [see abstract 2004. *American Mineralogist* 89: 469].

Orlandi, P., and M. Pasero 2006. Allanite-(La) from Buca della Vena mine, Apuan Alps, Italy, an epidote group mineral, *Canadian Mineralogist* 44 (1): 63-8.

Palache, C. 1935. The minerals of Franklin and Sterling Hill, Sussex County, New Jersey, *Geological Survey Professional Paper 180*, p. 98, [reprinted 1974 by Franklin-Ogdensburg Mineralogical Society].

Pautov, L., P. Khorov, K. Ignatenko, E. Sokolova, and T. Nadezhina, T. 1993. Khristovite-(Ce), a new mineral in the epidote group, *Zap. Vser. mineral. obshch.* 122 (3): 103-11 [in Russian; see abstract in Mandarino, J. 1997. *New Minerals 1990-1994*, Tucson: The Mineralogical Record, Inc.]

Pemberton, H. E. 1983. *Minerals of California*, New York: Van Nostrand Reinhold.

Peterson, O., K. Secher, and W. Bich 2006. Allanite-(Ce) and its type locality, *Rocks & Minerals* 81 (3): 200-5.

Poli, S., and M. W. Schmidt 2004. Experimental subsolidus studies on epidote minerals, *Reviews in Mineralogy and Geochemistry* 56: 171-95.

Shepel', A., and M. Karpenko 1969. Mukhinite, a new vanadium variety of epidote, *Doklady Akad. Nauk* 185 (6): 1342-5 [in Russian; see Pekov, I. 1998. *Minerals First Discovered on the Territory of the Former Soviet Union*, Moscow: Ocean Pictures].

Tumiati, S., G. Godard, S. Martin, and P. Nimis 2005. Dissakisite-(La), a new end-member of the epidote group from the Ulten peridotites (Italian Eastern Alps): Evidence of mantle-crust interactions in subduction zones, *Geophysical Research Abstracts*, Vol. 7, 00616.

Tumiati, S., S. Carbonin, V. Mair, and U. Russo 2006. Dissakisite-(La), Nuova specie dalla Val d'Ultimo, Alto Adige, *Rivista Mineralogica Italiana* 4/2006, 244-49.